AMAZING
AUSTRALIA

The Broad Arrow Tavern (above) *is a typical outback pub near Kalgoorlie in Western Australia.*

Contents

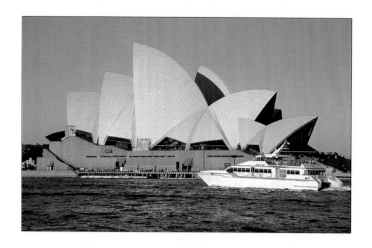

NEW SOUTH WALES

New South Wales deserves its prized sobriquet, the 'Premier State', as a third of Australia's population lives there. It is also the most preferred destination for overseas and interstate visitors – the climate is temperate and there is an abundantly diverse landscape ranging from craggy mountains to rolling plains, semi-arid deserts and pristine beaches lying amidst a rugged coastline. New South Wales also has one of the most magnificent settings for its capital city, Sydney. The celebrated harbour is hemmed in by sand-stone headlands with 60km of the Pacific coast forming the city's eastern perimeter. Sydney was the birthplace of European settlement in Australia and from the first tentative years of the British colony through to independence in 1901, and onwards across the 20th century, it has witnessed and shaped many of the major events of modern Australia.

The 'Coat-Hanger', as the Sydney Harbour Bridge (right) *is often known, and the serrated sails of the Opera House* (above) *are twin symbols of Sydney,* ① *the place where European settlement began.*

The annual Australia Day Ferry Race (above) *is one of Sydney's most festive events. Watched by spectators on tall and small ships alike, it takes place on 26 January.*

Darling Harbour (top) is Sydney's mid-city escape hatch. A sprawling development of dramatic glass architecture, it boasts scores of restaurants, souvenir boutiques and bars.

Sydney's beaches are a paradise for surfers, joggers and swimmers. Manly (above) lies at the bottom of the slope coming down from North Head. Bondi (opposite) is Australia's most celebrated beach and is tucked between rugged headlands south of the city centre. On Bondi promenade there is a skateboard ramp where young speed fiends (above) can burn off energy.

The historic Rocks (above) is a remnant of the original Sydney Town. It is a maze of alleys with sufficient pubs, galleries and waterfront restaurants to keep any visitor entertained.

5

The rugged Blue Mountains, ② west of Sydney, form part of the Great Dividing Range. In Katoomba ③ the Skyway passes Orphan Rock (top) and offers stunning views over the Jamison Valley. The majestic Three Sisters (right) can be seen from Echo Point. Evan's Lookout (centre) is the start of the three-hour Grand Canyon Walk traversing the Grose Valley. South-west of Katoomba, the limestone Jenolan Caves ④ (above) are full of wonderfully lit formations.

All along the northern coastline of New South Wales, from Tweed Heads at the Queensland border to Broken Bay, just north of Sydney, seaside resorts offer excellent facilities for holidaymakers. Two of the most well-known are Coffs Harbour and Port Macquarie. The breakwater protecting the jetty in Coffs Harbour ⑤ (above) is wholly man-made and links the mainland to Muttonbird Island. On this drab, heath-like limb thousands of migratory shearwaters converge to breed in the southern summer. Settlement City (left) on the Hastings River at Port Macquarie ⑥ is a large shopping complex, which includes the Tavern on the Pier where visitors can try their luck with slot machines or catch an entertainment act after a hard day on the beach.

Southern New South Wales includes such enticements as the tranquil Southern Highlands, the exhilarating sport resorts in the Snowy Mountains and the isolated beaches of the southern coast. Perisher Valley (opposite), like all the New South Wales ski resorts, is within the Kosciusko National Park. ⑦ The snow season starts at the beginning of June and lasts for about four months. During the summer, the area is perfect for trail-bike riding, hang-gliding, camping, and bushwalking. Blenheim Beach (left) at Jervis Bay ⑧ is a beautiful place to escape the bustle of the world. Its sandy beach and azure blue waters are protected within the enfolding arm of the Beecroft Peninsula.

AUSTRALIAN CAPITAL TERRITORY

Canberra lies at the heart of the Australian Capital Territory (ACT). The 2360km^2 excised from New South Wales in 1908 is home to politicians, public servants, diplomats, and academics. The city was designed in 1912 by Walter Burley Griffin and his original plan of boulevards and focal points is clearly evident. The old Parliament House, opened in 1927, is now the National Portrait Gallery. The unusual design of the new Parliament House comprises a sloped grass roof to allow visitors to clamber over the top of the federal seat of power. There are many surprising buildings in Canberra, including the embassies which reflect the traditional cultures of the occupants. The city also has superb parklands, the picturesque man-made Lake Burley Griffin and numerous art and cultural centres of excellence.

Parliament House (above) *in Canberra* ⑨ *was completed in 1988. Poised on the other side of the lake is the Australian War Memorial* (below). *Sculptures, like this elegant bronze lady* (below left), *are a feature of the cityscape. Hot-air balloons* (right) *provide a perfect way to see Griffin's vision.*

Surfers Paradise ⑩ (above) on the Gold Coast is famous for the intensity of its nightlife, its vast stretch of white beach and its endless choice of waves.

There are seven bridges that straddle the Brisbane River as it meanders through the city, the most famous being the Story Bridge (above).

QUEENSLAND

Queensland is Australia's 'Sunshine State', a place of beaches, rainforests, deserts, Aboriginal culture, and modern cities. With an area of 1.7 million km² and 7400km of coastline, its statistics are a little overwhelming. In fact, Queensland is so large that it occupies almost one-quarter of the Australian continent. Its main tourist centres are on the coast, principally in the south-eastern corner and the far north. The Great Barrier Reef, with its offshore islands, has become one of the most popular holiday destinations. It is both the largest coral reef in the world and the planet's largest living organism. The reef stretches some 2000km along the coast, from the tip of Cape York to Bundaberg in the south, and is home to an astonishing number of coral, fish and crustaceans as well as mammals like dolphins and whales. Queensland has 540 continental islands and hundreds more cays. Some islands are still much the same as they were when Captain James Cook sailed past in 1770. The ancestors of Queensland's Aborigines and Torres Strait Islanders are believed to have migrated to the area more than 40 000 years ago. Today, the state has a large multicultural population with strong regional variations which range from the cosmopolitan people of the south-east to the rural ways of the outback.

The Gold Coast ⑪ (above), an hour's drive from Brisbane, is a glittering strip of beaches with a number of wild-life parks nearby, as well as the popular theme parks of Sea World, Dreamworld and Warner Bros. Movie World. Brisbane ⑫ (opposite), Queensland's sunny capital, sprawls along the banks of the river of the same name.

Cooloola National Park, ⑬ just north of Noosa ⑭ on the Sunshine Coast, is home to the Teewah Coloured Sands (left). These 200m-high cliffs comprise more than 70 different colours and create a spectacular vista beside the white sands of the beach.

Fraser Island ⑮ (left) is the largest sand island in the world and is World Heritage-listed. There are numerous camping sites, including this one beside Lake Boomanjin, the world's largest above-sea-level lake 'perched' in the dunes.

Many parts of the island are only accessible by four-wheel-drive including the beautiful Champagne pools (below). The broadwalks at Central Station (right) allow visitors to experience old-growth forest which has grown on top of the sand.

Queensland has many wonderful locations where the Great Barrier Reef's ⑯ *extraordinary variety of sea life (opposite) can be experienced. Offshore from Cairns, Green Island* ⑰ *offers the chance to enjoy clear underwater views from the Yellow Submarine (below). From the mainland and the islands of the Whitsunday Group, boats travel to the outer reef where sharks and giant manta rays can be seen as well as delicate species like the red-fin butterfly fish (right). Whitsunday Island has been preserved as a national park and the heavenly Whitehaven Beach* ⑱ *(bottom) can be reached by boat or by seaplane.*

Cool and tranquil Mossman Gorge (above) in the Daintree National Park ⑲ seems aeons from the bustle of Cairns. The Daintree and Cape Tribulation ⑳ national parks are within the Wet Tropics World Heritage area.

In Kuranda ㉑ the members of the remarkable Tjapukai Aboriginal Dance Theatre (left) present a corroboree which combines their local lore and legends with contemporary jokes, music and animal mime.

The village of Kuranda nestles in the mountain range behind Cairns. The train journey (above) between the two towns zigzags up the incline – which offers stunning views of the rainforest, over the Barron Falls and out across the Coral Sea.

The Mossman and Daintree rivers carve their way through the rainforested region of the national parks. Many of their tributaries, like Oliver Creek (above), open up pathways so that ancient trees and, perhaps, rare wildlife can be seen.

One of the most distinctive forms of transport in the Australian outback is the road train (above). This is a series of heavy articulated trailers pulled by a powerful prime mover.

Daly Waters ㉒ began life when the Overland Telegraph Line was being laid in the 1870s; the pub's decor (above) reflects the sense of humour needed to survive in the outback.

Katatjuta ㉓ (above), meaning 'many heads', and Uluru ㉔ (left), a giant sandstone mass 10km in girth, were formerly known as the Olgas and Ayers Rock respectively. These two distinctive landforms of the Northern Territory are sacred Aboriginal sites.

NORTHERN TERRITORY

The Northern Territory, known as the Top End, is a combination of arid land and fertile wilderness, sparsely populated with around 170 000 people. Outposts of civilisation, such as mining towns, vast cattle stations, Aboriginal settlements and the occasional petrol station, are complemented by lush World Heritage tropical zones. The territory covers 1.3 million km², from the Arafura Sea to the 'Red Centre' or 'Dead Heart'. Alice Springs, virtually at the geographical centre of the continent, nestles at the foot of the MacDonnell Ranges and, beyond that, the desert stretches out in all directions. This area is rich in outback history and Aboriginal culture. Some 1500km north, through a landscape mostly occupied by kangaroos, anthills, endless scrub, and thundering road trains, lies the capital, Darwin. The city was entirely rebuilt after it was flattened by a tropical cyclone on Christmas Eve in 1974. Nearby (in Australian terms at least) is Kakadu National Park, a 20 000km² kingdom of forests, flood plains and ancient Aboriginal art.

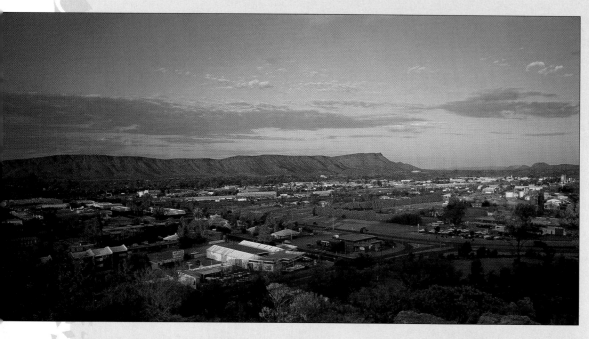

One of the nicknames given to the outback, the 'Red Centre', seems
apt when looking at the countryside surrounding Alice Springs ㉕ (top).
The MacDonnell Ranges, ㉖ seen in the background, contain many special
hideaways including Ormiston Gorge (above left) which twists its way
between the multi-hued sheer walls of the range.

Nearby, at the Pitchi Ritchi Sanctuary, William Ricketts expresses the
stories of the Aboriginal Dreamtime in his sculptures (above) and, by blend-
ing them into the landscape, depicts the Aborigines' attachment to the land.

The old stone buildings at the repeater station at Alice Springs (right)
have been restored to preserve the history of the Morse-code-driven Overland
Telegraph Line which opened much of this outback territory to the world.

Some 365km north of Alice are the Devils Marbles ㉗ (above), *a cluster of granite boulders which Aborigines once believed to be the eggs of the legendary Rainbow Serpent.*

The streets of Tennant Creek ㉘ (left) *may look deserted but, with a population of 3500, it is both one of the largest and most isolated towns in the territory.*

The 130-year-old Gold Stamp Battery near Tennant Creek (left) *has been turned into a museum where conducted tours enable visitors to see the processes of goldmining and how the crushing and stamping plant operated.*

The Katherine Gorge National Park, ㉙ 'down the track' from Darwin, *has a series of spectacular sandstone cliffs rising above the Katherine River (left), a perfect place for canoeing.*

Springvale, ㉚ which is near Katherine, *offers visitors the chance to see traditional Aboriginal corroboree dances (right) that comprise part of celebration ceremonies held on special occasions.*

25

The Kakadu National Park ㉛ contains ancient Aboriginal rock images like the 'Lightning Man' (left) at Nourlangie Rock. It is also a haven for a myriad flora and fauna, such as magpie geese, jabiru and brolga birds. The best way to see wetland areas like Yellow Waters (opposite) is by boat.

Darwin, ㉜ the capital of the Territory, has a tropical climate and comprises a large multicultural population. A favourite pastime is the rodeo (above) where bronco riding and steer wrestling thrill both locals and visitors. In contrast, Fanny Bay (below) reflects the relaxed atmosphere of the city.

WESTERN AUSTRALIA

Enormous, mineral-rich Western Australia has 1 million fewer people than its 2.5 million km² of land and ranges from the arid to the fertile, modern to old. Two-thirds of the population live in Perth, a capital that has grown confident and prosperous in the last three decades. South of Perth is the port of Fremantle whose convict-era buildings contrast with the high-rises of the capital. Fremantle's waters are famous for yachting. The south-west region of the state contains wineries, caves, heritage trails, forests of jarrah and kauri pine and the picturesque town of Albany. Heading north, the unusual Wave Rock at Hyden introduces the rugged terrain where towns like Kalgoorlie sprang to life in the gold rush of the last century. The national parks of Kalbarri, Nambung and Purnululu possess many unique landforms: stunning gorges, the unearthly Pinnacles and the beehive-shaped Bungle Bungle massif. Along the dramatic and dangerous coastline, pearl harvesting still operates at Broome and the waves crash onto the isolated and spectacular beaches and headlands.

Located on the Swan River, it is hard to believe that Perth ③③ (opposite) is one of the most remote cities on earth. The bushland reserve of Kings Park (below) presents nature at its unadorned best. Rottnest Island ③④ (bottom) is 19km from the coast and is home to the quokka (below right), a small relative of the kangaroo.

Nature's Window (above) *lies within Kalbarri National Park* ㉟ *which supports over 300 species of flowering plant, like the verticordia (below left).*

Hawke's Head (above) *is a gorge where the rock formation has been carved by the Murchison River which winds through the Kalbarri. This national park is on the coast to the north of Perth and is famed for its multicoloured cliffs, dramatic gorges and exceptionally rich wildflower displays.*

Out of the dunefields and sandplains of the Nambung National Park, ㊱ *south of Kalbarri, rise the Pinnacles* (below). *These protruding sandstone spires are thought to have been formed around the roots of ancient desert plants, creating strange shapes on the landscape.*

Wave Rock ③⑦ *(above) is located some 350km inland from Perth at the small township of Hyden. The 15m-high, hollow granite face that gives the rock its name was carved over the millennia by wind erosion.*

Broome ㊳ started in the 1870s when Japanese pearl fishers discovered a rich cache; gravestones (left) recall these early divers. Pearling luggers (top) carry tourists in Roebuck Bay. Cable Beach (far left) can be explored on camel-back. Petrified dinosaur footprints can be seen at Gantheaume Bay (centre). The Bungle Bungles (bottom) are in Purnululu National Park. ㊵

SOUTH AUSTRALIA

South Australia, like much of the country, is full of contrasts: from Adelaide's geometric 1836 town plan to outback opal-mining communities like Coober Pedy, to picturesque coastal spots and extensive waterways – notably the mighty Murray River. The Flinders Ranges and Kangaroo Island are probably the state's best known features while the Barossa Valley produces 75 per cent of Australia's wine. South Australia was the first state to be founded by free settlers and an extensive German influence is evident in places like Hahndorf and Kaiser Stuhl. The ancient Flinders Ranges are at their most dramatic in the northern desert region around Wilpena Pound, a giant quartzite amphitheatre and South Australia's most outstanding geographical feature. Adelaide sits on a coastal plain beside the Gulf of St. Vincent and is also known as the 'City of Light' in honour of its designer, Colonel William Light.

Adelaide ④⓪ is a city of churches as is evident by the many spires (above left). *A dramatic fountain* (above right) *graces Victoria Square in the central district. The River Torrens* (right) *is flanked by parklands and the white-roofed Festival Centre. Kangaroo Island ④① has many wilderness areas, like the Bluff at Kingscote* (below), *where the wildlife that gave the island its name can hop freely.*

The Flinders Ranges National Park ㊷ is wild and defiantly unspoilt. Rocky outcrops, like St Mary's Peak (top) overlooking the Bunyeroo Valley, rise between the deep gorges. The vineyards of the Barossa Valley ㊸ (above) create many of Australia's premier wines and welcome visitors for wine tastings and sales. The outback town of Coober Pedy ㊹ is famous for white opals and subterranean living, which allows the 2000 residents to escape the fierce temperatures. Even the churches are built underground (left).

This handful of opals (left) is part of the Opal Cave collection and is worth around A$180 000.

VICTORIA

Victoria comprises only three per cent of the Australian landmass but enjoys an excellent blend of climate and natural resources. Framed by the Murray River, South Australia and the ocean, the landscape moves from semi-desert to fertile woodlands, from snowfields to cradle lakes, from bustling cities to rugged coastlines. Its capital, Melbourne, established in 1835, is the continent's second-largest city. The Yarra River winds through the historic CBD where many grand Victorian buildings exhibit the mid-19th-century gold-rush wealth. Today, Melbourne is still a thriving capital priding itself on its culture.

Four great icons of Melbourne ㊺ are its city trams (top); the pubs and coffee bars of Lygon Street (centre); the Yarra River which flows under the elegant Princes Bridge (above); and the magnificent Botanic Gardens (left).

*A conservation and exhibition centre (above) has been set up
on Phillip Island ㊻ where visitors flock to see the nightly fairy
penguin parade (below left).*

*The Puffing Billy (below) has been in service for over 100 years
and travels through lush bushland affording fabulous views of
the Dandenong Ranges. ㊼*

*One of Victoria's most popular tourist excursions are the Twelve
Apostles ㊽ (right) at Port Campbell National Park. ㊾ These
weathered pillars were once part of the mainland.*

The frantic 1850s gold rushes of Ballarat ⑤⓪ are recreated at the Sovereign Hill Historical Park. The poppet head (above) of the old mine dominates the site as it hauls dirt up from beneath the surface. Visitors to the park are also encouraged to pan for gold.

Rising sheer from the plains, the Grampian Ranges ⑤① hide many splendid walking trails, valleys, cliffs and waterfalls, such as the lush McKenzie Falls (above).

In Sovereign Hill (above) coaches clatter past the old-world shops that help recreate the ambience of the gold-rush times. Halls Gap Lookout (left) is one of the dramatic peaks that dominate the craggy Grampian Ranges. There are more than 100 sacred Aboriginal rock-art sites within the Grampians (called Gariwerd by the local Aborigines).

Possums, quolls and the feisty Tasmanian devil (right) are all common in the remote high country of Tasmania.

TASMANIA

Tasmania was originally known as Van Diemen's Land (after the Dutch navigator who first sighted its coast) and after 1803 as 'hell on earth' due to the savage British penal colony established there. Today, you're more likely to hear it called 'the apple isle'. The state capital, Hobart, has managed to combine much of its early architectural heritage with its modern additions, like the Wrest Point Casino (the first legal casino in Australia), to create a city with charm. Mount Wellington (1270m) and the equally imposing Mount Nelson form a spectacular backdrop to the capital. The former Port Arthur prison colony, built in 1842 and housing over 600 prisoners, is now a peaceful tourist attraction. Tasmania's rugged interior is home to Cradle Mountain–Lake St Clair National Park and the 1443m Frenchmans Cap – the highest peak in the island's extensive World Heritage area.

Port Arthur ⑤² (right) was once a brutal penal settlement but is now one of Tasmania's most popular tourist sites with tranquil lawns.

Hobart (above) ⑤³ huddles close to the Derwent River and the Wrest Point Casino dominates the foreshore development. Peaceful fishing trawlers berth at Constitution Dock (right), but once a year their haven is invaded by the ocean-racing yachts who finish the Sydney to Hobart race.

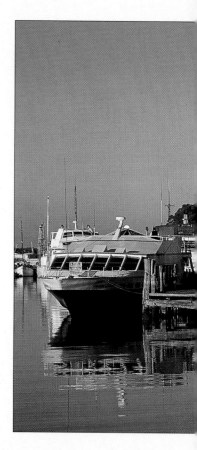

Cradle Mountain–Lake St Clair National Park ⑤④ is a World Heritage area which comprises rugged mountains, glacial lakes, wild alpine moorlands, and forested valleys. During the winter months, however, the snow can make driving hazardous (right). On the west coast of Tasmania boats shelter in Macquarie Harbour (below) where the tiny picturesque town of Strahan ⑤⑤ is located.

Strahan (above) *is the access point to the Gordon River, which runs through the Franklin-Gordon Wild Rivers National Park. These rivers provide the most challenging rafting waterways in Australia. Seaplanes (left) are perhaps the best way to grasp the size of Macquarie Harbour,* 56 *one of the largest natural harbours in the world. Enclosed by thick forested mountains, the entrance is called Hells Gates because of its dangerous sandbars and rips.*

(Following page) *The Penny Royal Complex at Launceston* 57 *retains the beauty of the town's historical past.*

First published in 1996
Reprinted 1998
New Holland Publishers Pty Ltd
London • Cape Town • Sydney • Singapore

Produced in Australia by
New Holland Publishers
3/2 Aquatic Drive, Frenchs Forest
NSW 2086, Australia

24 Nutford Place
London W1H 6DQ
United Kingdom

80 McKenzie Street
Cape Town 8001
South Africa

PHOTOGRAPHIC CREDITS

Copyright © in photographs: **NHIL** (Shaen Adey) with the exception of the following: **APL** (F. Prenzel): p40 (inset); **Chris Clark** (Images of Adelaide): p37 (centre); **Coo-ee Picture Library**: front cover (main), p42; **Coo-ee Picture Library** (Ron Ryan): p41; **Kevin Deacon** (Ocean Earth Images): pp16, 17 (inset), back cover (main & inset); **David McGonigal**: p31; **Nature Focus Australian Museum**: p44 (inset); **NHIL**: pp6 (top & bottom), 8, 22 (bottom left & right), 40 (bottom), 43 (top left & right, & bottom), 48; **NHIL** (Anthony Johnson): front cover (top centre), pp3, 5 (top & bottom), 10 (top, bottom & inset), 11, 12, 13 (bottom), 17 (bottom), 19 (bottom right), 20, 21 (bottom), 22 (top), 23, 28, 29 (top), 34 (top left & right), 35, 38, 39 (inset, top & bottom), 44 (bottom), 45, 46 (bottom), 47 (top & bottom); **NHIL** (Nick Rains): pp2 (top), 4, 5 (centre & inset), 7; **Mark Rajkovic** (Shoot Pty Ltd.): p44 (top)
APL = Australian Picture Library • NHIL = New Holland Image Library.

Writer: John Borthwick
Designer and Typesetter: Alix Gracie
Publishing Manager: Mariëlle Renssen
Commissioning Editor: Sally Bird
Editors: Joanne Holliman, Jane Maliepaard & Anouska Good
Picture Researcher: Vicki Hastrich
Cartographer: John Loubser
Reproduction: Unifoto (Pty) Ltd
Printed and bound in Singapore by Tien Wah Press (Pte) Ltd